WHICH COMPONENTS?

The components to make a 10s battery pack are simple and very intuitive to use, we have:

1 **10S control card with multi-cable connector**
1 **set of electric cables of power and medium power**
10 **18650 lithium cells (or multiples of 10 where necessary to parallel)**
1 **10S mains charger**
2 **plastic sockets' for 10S**
1 **set of nickel conductor for welding the cells**
1 **connector for charging**
2 **power connector (Output for load) 1M / 1F**
1 **Thermal jacket to close the package - OPTIONAL**

We recommend using a good quality rubberized electric cable, this type of product is flexible, resistant and highly insulating, as well as giving you a very high electrical conductivity, which as we know is the focal point of lithium batteries, in fact only one cell is capable of generating very high peak currents, even over 20 amperes. If not of good quality the cable will go into combustion at the first sign of overcurrent.

Let's see in detail the basic components of this battery pack, we inform you however that there are hundreds of alternatives to go to make a 10S battery pack, with more or less components and accessories.

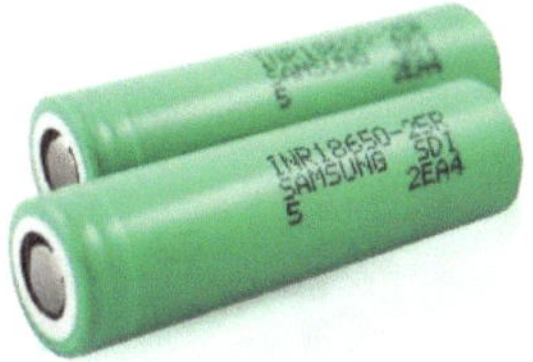

Example of charge adjustment card for 10s battery pack

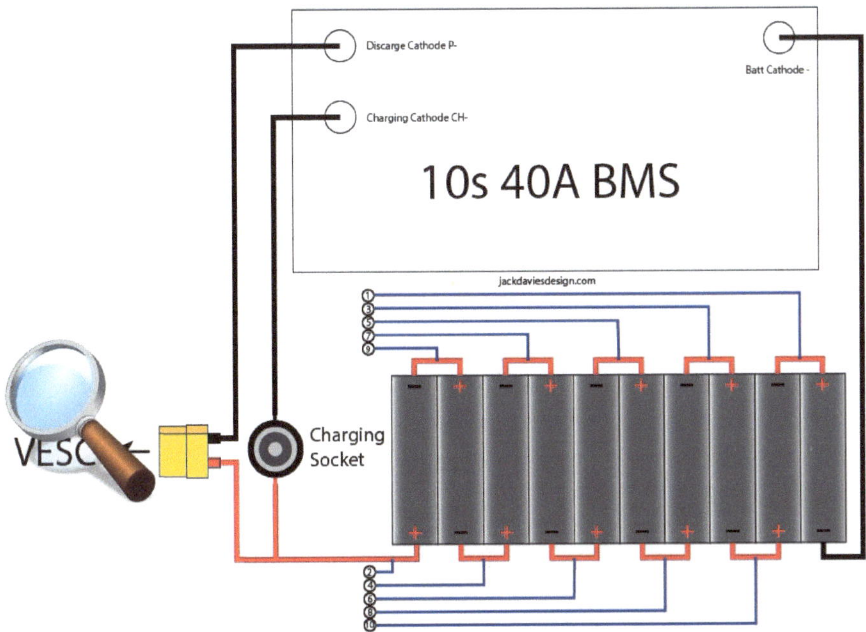

There are different control and charge balancing units on the market, how can we distinguish which one is right for us? In the case of a 10-cell battery pack in series and with a final voltage of about 36V we must necessarily go and buy a card made for this purpose. In Photo the 10S card, small in size but precise and very reliable, thanks to the various integrated protections, see temperature protection, overload protection, short circuit and low charger (low cell voltage). In fact we have the system that protects the cells from a charge beyond the threshold and from a discharge below the threshold. Another important fact to choose the board is the maximum output current, in fact this board has a maximum output current of about 15A, this is a given as we said important because based on what we have to go to feed the board must be chosen. The more our load absorbs current, the more our charge balancing card will allow proper charging of the same. If you need to power a max 42V circuit with low power consumption, you can choose a BMS card with low current, but the more power is used, the higher the card must be.The card as you will have understood by now, does a double job, that of recharging the cells, in fact it will recharge in a distinct and separate manner the 10 cells that you have welded in series, this thanks to the interconnections with the BMS wiring, Each cell will recharge up to the threshold of about 4.2v and not below about 2.9v when discharged. The task of the card will be to keep the cells at the same voltage throughout the life of the battery pack. The second job of the card is to manage the power load, therefore supplying electricity to your user, managing current peaks and possibly protecting from various external and internal effects on the battery pack.

ATTENTION: When you go to weld the cells pay maximum attention not to invert the polarities, lithium batteries with high explosive power

WHICH ELECTRICAL SCHEME

How can you see the 10S system are 10 18650 batteries welded in series, this system can be used both with 10 cells and with multiple cells (parallel) See example below.

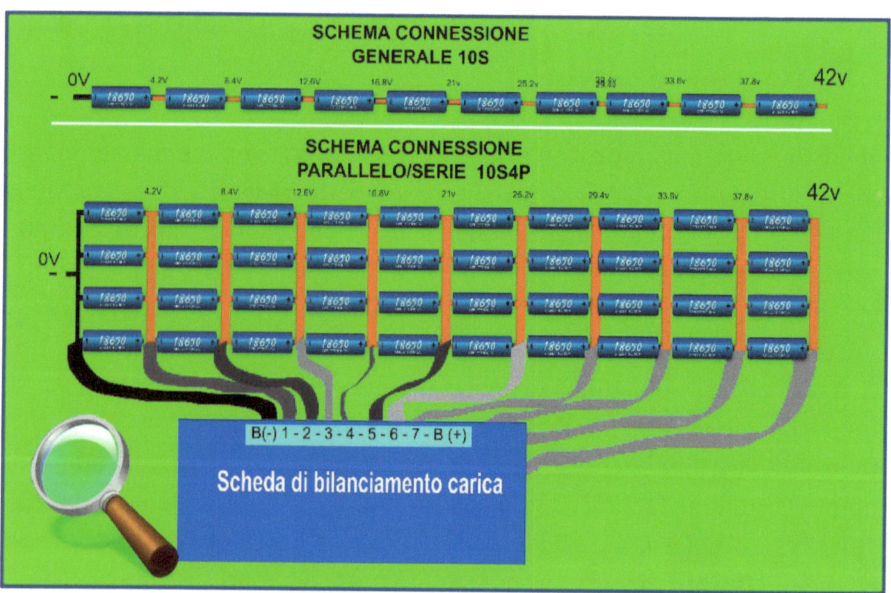

The power supply to feed your loads will be taken from the pads of your management card, according to the board differentiate the PAD.

You will still have:

2 pads for the battery (positive / negative) plus all the intermediate sectors, which are the connection points between the series.
2 pads for the charger
2 pads for the user power output

Many regulators, on the other hand, have fewer pads, this because they share the input and output by unifying them in just two PADs, so you will have two pads for charging / output Voltage inputs and another two for the battery connection.

The 10S System can be zoomed almost infinitely, where it is necessary to install more cells in parallel, which obviously have the same capacity or with small differences. To help you build your lithium cell battery pack, we recommend you visit this site. It is an ONLINE calculator that will allow you to balance your battery packs starting from the various cell capacities.

Click here http://repackr.com/

How does this useful tool called REPACKR work?
Repackr is nothing more than an online software dedicated to the lovers of lithium and battery technology.
Just enter in the first field the various values of the cells you have available, for example we simulate going to make a 3S battery pack with 12 lithium cells at our disposal. In the first field called '' Cells '' we are going to write separated by comma the various values of our cells (the ones we write on the body of the cell) that we remind you of. GFE can supply you with 18650 tested cells, with TOP values and capacity, at very low prices competitive, exclusive Samsung, Sony, Sanyo, Panasonic cells, and many other quality brands.

Step1: WE INSERT THE CAPACITY VALUES OF OUR 12 CELLS (the 3s3P package will have only 9 cells)
Step2: WE SPECIFY IN THE PROGRAM WHICH TYPE OF BATTERY PACKAGE WE WANT TO BUILD, IN THE SPECIFIC AS MANY SERIES AND HOW MANY PARALLELS. Our case as per premise is 3 Series and 3 Parallels.
After filling in the 3 fields, just click on the Generate Packs button, this will generate the best solution in a few seconds to create the 3 parallel cells that you will then weld in series. In a nutshell the program calculates the cells in such a way as to install them in such combination as to have a similar Mah capacity as possible. Because as we know we cannot put cells or parallels with remarkably different capacities in series.

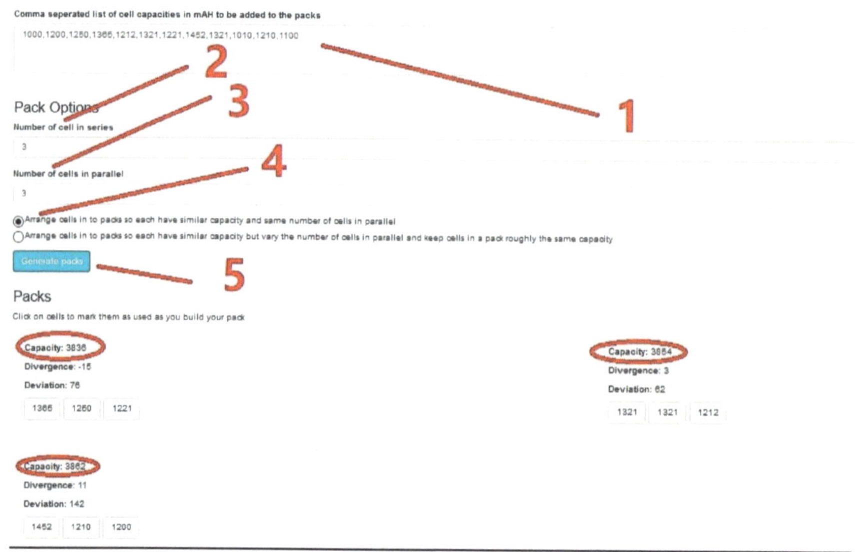

As you can see from this example, even though our cells are of different capacities, in the end the software allowed us to create 3 parallel numbers from about 3800mah (3836 - 3854 - 3862). In this case as you can see starting from loose cells and making no confusion at the time of welding, we have the opportunity to make a stable battery pack and give us good performance, as well as not giving us problems with the charge balancing card, which will I remember from the time of welding and the first start, all the cells must be at the same value of times with capacity of each parallel as close as possible, this example that we have just seen differs between one and the other of about 11mA, which is a negligible value.

The 12 cells we calculated are these

1000,1200,1250,1365,1212,1321,1221,1452,1321,1010,1210,1100

All completely different but then the program gave us as a result:

Parallel 1 capacity: 3836mah

Cells to be used: 1365/1250/1221

Parallel 2 capacity: 3854mah

Cells to be used: 1321/1321/1212

Parallel 3 capacity: 3862mah

Cells to be used: 1452/1210/1200

PRESENT A LOT OF ATTENTION TO THIS PHASE, EVERY ERROR IN THE DESIGN OF PARALLELS RELUCKS TO THE ACTUAL OPERATION OF YOUR BATTERY PACKAGE.

After having subdivided the 12 cells as recommended by our super program, we can start to weld the cells. I recommend that the groups of cells that the program creates are all welded in parallel. They are all groups of cells of 4.2v (not wrong to connect them in series). The parallel connection is the ++ / - connection.

Our simulated battery pack after finishing the cell welding, installation of the charge balancing board and the recharging connector, also the bipolar electric cable for the connection to our user will have these characteristics:

12v battery pack

Total capacity: 3.8ah

Voltage: 12.6v

Max Out current (depending on your BMS we simulate 12A)

Cell number: 12

Plug-in connectors for BMS

 These are some of the connectors for charge balancing cards, as you can see there are as many models as there are battery pack models that can be built. The color of the electric wires can obviously vary, there are those only dyed, those two-tone, those like in red and black or still numbered ones. We advise you to pay attention when inserting into the BMS connector, this connector has a very specific direction, if you try to insert it on the contrary it DOES NOT enter, therefore DO NOT insist because you risk breaking the connector and the welds on the BMS card. I remind you that the two external cables are NEGATIVE and the other is the total POSITIVE of your battery pack. Those in the middle are the various '' series 'connections.

THE STEP FOR THE CONSTRUCTION:

After making (soldered) the various parallels of your battery pack that we advise you to do in the most professional way possible, see our guide (Techniques for welding 18650 lithium batteries for € 9.90)
Prepare the balancing board, for battery packs like yours, that is, with more than one cell in series, you will have to weld various electric cables, as many as there are series connections between cell and cell. In addition, on the card itself, go and solder the cell recharging cable and another "exit" cable. We advise you to make your battery pack using only cells that have already been tested and are working with suitable output voltages. In addition, before welding them, it is good practice to ensure that cells per cell have similar voltages. The best charge balancing cards have a plug-in connector kidnapped with already encapsulated electric cables (about 10 / 25cm) each, these wires are the veins of our battery, in fact from these cables will pass the current of each sector, and thanks to these the battery pack will be balanced.

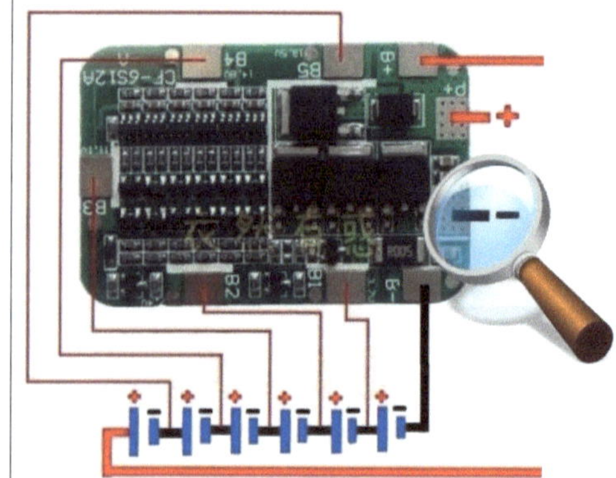

The BMS is interconnected to the cells via these electric cables, which I highly recommend MAKE ATTENTION. It has a starting order, in the sense that they should not be soldered randomly but you have to weld the cables from the one named B (-) step by step to that B (+). Any error made in this step will cause irreparable damage to the load balancing card.

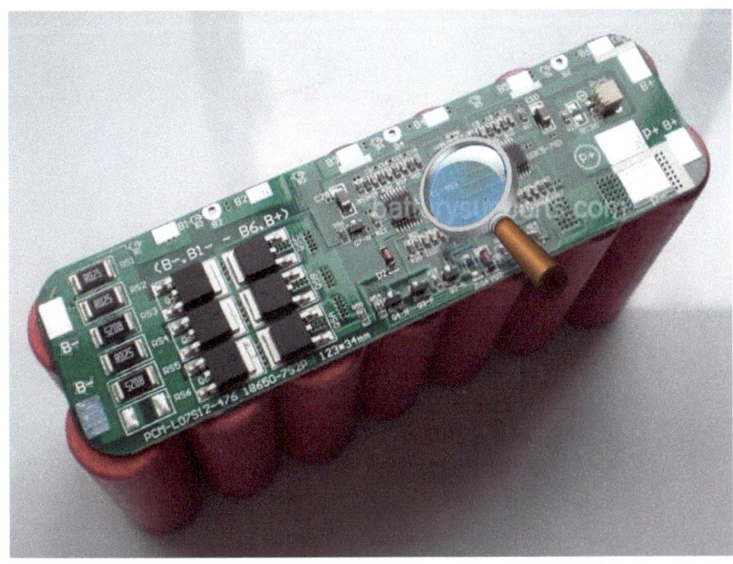

Example 10 Series cells for 3 Parallel

Seen from the top of a battery pack on the front and back side, pay attention to how they are assembled, one of the two sides has the positive pole on the edges and the general negative on the other.

FRONT BATTERY PACK:

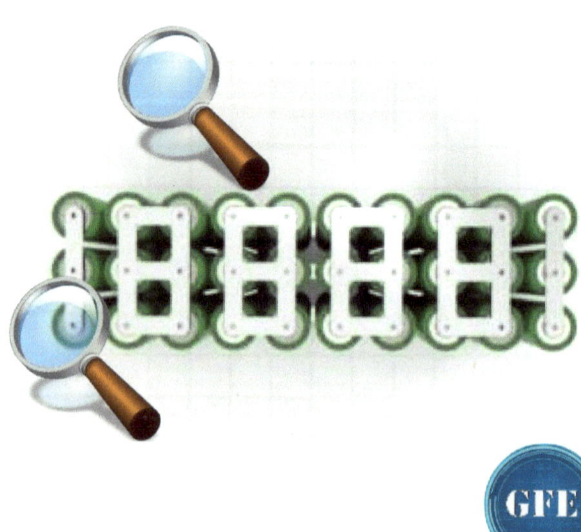

BACK BATTERY PACK:

HOW THE BATTERY IS TESTED:

The battery test must pay attention to any strangeness in operation, both as regards the heat generated by the components and by the "stability of the whole system". Everything must work in a linear, continuous and without phases contact. After checking that you have made no errors in the connections and everything seems to work, go and measure the various voltages with a tester, those of the cell (in the case of **10S**) you have to measure cell by cell in series plus those output to the board (where it uses a card with part OUT).

The voltages you MUST HAVE *: 0v - 4.2v - 8.4v - 12.6v - 16.8v - 21v - 25.2v - 29.4v - 33.6V - 37.8V - 42V

* You will have these voltage values only if all the cells are charged to the maximum, where instead the cells are not, it is normal that the voltages offset less than these values, but the important thing is that by doing the calculations you always have the correct voltages in the sector by sector (series by series). To go and connect your load, I suggest you to use a quality electric cable, this will need to be soldered on the various PADs on the board, some balancing boards have only the NEGATIVE on PAD, the POSITIVE must be taken directly from the battery pack (final cell with positive pole) This is because the board goes to work and close where necessary (in case of tripping protection ends, short circuit, overload) the negative pole, having the positive pole directly connected to your load.

Finally, when we confirm that our battery pack works optimally, both as a discharge and as a charge, the time has come to secure the components, the best solution is to use our plastic stockings, just insert the battery inside and heat it with a hair dryer, in a few seconds the battery pack will be insulated, and the components will be safe from splashes and possible accesses of metal bodies (short circuits).

If you use quality management cards you do not need fuses inside the battery, as the electronics will act as internal protection, but a suggestion I give you is to put the fuse OUT of the battery, that is on the POSITIVE cable out of the battery, pay close attention to which one you use, danger of cable fire and card in cases where a correct fuse has not been inserted.

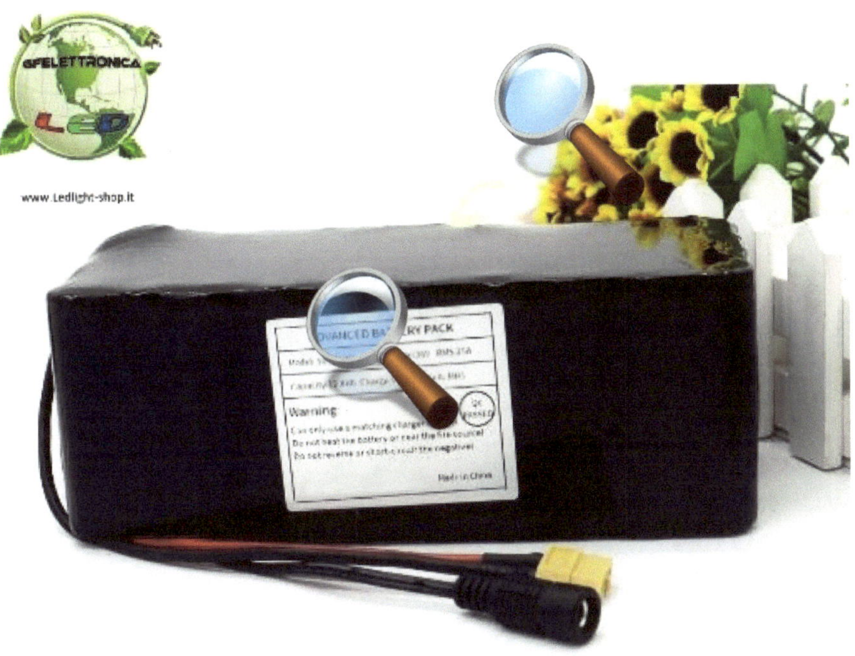

WHAT NOT TO DO DURING THE CONSTRUCTION OF A LITHIUM BATTERY PACK:

NEVER INVERT A CELL OR MORE DURING THE PARALLEL WELDING
DO NOT USE CELLS WITH VOLTAGE UNDER THE 2.4V
DO NOT USE CELLS WITH RIPPED PROTECTIVE FILM
DO NOT WELD THE CELLS WITHOUT THE PROTECTIVE PAD ON THE POSITIVE POLE
DO NOT SHORTEN DURING THE WELDING OF THE POSITIVE POLE
DO NOT POUND OVER POND ON POSITIVE POLE (IMMEDIATE SHORT CIRCUIT CAUSE)
DO NOT INVERT THE BMS INTERCONNECTION LEADS
DO NOT MISTAKE TO CONNECT THE BMS TO THE BMS
DO NOT SHORTEN THE CELLS WHILE YOU GO TO WELD
DO NOT WASH THE BATTERY
KEEP OUT OF REACH OF CHILDREN PACKAGE NOT PROTECTED
DO NOT KEEP THE SAME BATTERY WITHOUT A PROTECTIVE CONTAINER
DO NOT USE CABLES OF TOO SMALL SECTION
DO NOT USE LOW QUALITY CABINETS
DO NOT USE LOW QUALITY TIN

WHAT TO DO DURING THE CONSTRUCTION OF A LITHIUM BATTERY PACK:

TEST ALL THE CELLS ONE BY ONE BEFORE THE BEGINNING
USE ONLY CELLS PROTECTED BY FILM
USE ONLY CELLS WITH VOLTAGE> 3.7V
LOAD CELLS BEFORE 3.7V USE
USE A GOOD WELDING SYSTEM
USE A QUALITY POND

**USE WELDING POINTS IF YOU HAVE
PROTECT ELECTRIC CABLES TO THE MAXIMUM
THE WIRES IN OPTIMAL WAY
USE A PROTECTION FUSE IN THE POSITIVE EXIT POLE
CONNECT THE CONTROL UNIT CABLES IN A
MANUFACTURED AND CORRECT MANNER
POSITION THE BMS CONTROL UNIT IN SALDA MANIERA**

CONNECTORS plug?

Yes! Plug-in connectors are a standard in the world of electronics, home automation and DIY in general, in line with current regulations, these connectors can be used in low voltage, or for some models even in medium and high voltage. As the inrush currents vary, the connector model must obviously vary, since the higher the current the more the thickness of the metal connection part must be.
90% of the connectors on the market consist of a plastic body / abs with two conductive poles in the inner part, which are POSITIVE and NEGATIVE. What changes?
The shape of the connectors themselves changes, there will be the females and the males, and their union will be guaranteed by the plastic structure as well as by the metal of the poles that are self-engaged.

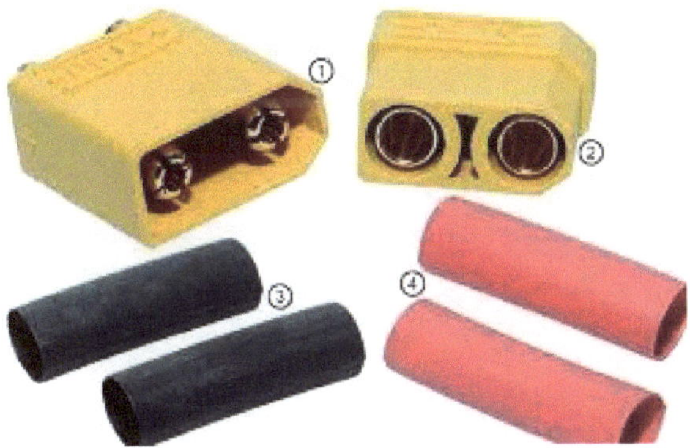

This is an example of a plug-in connector, perhaps the most widely used in robotics, drones, and lithium batteries. It is one of a series of similar connectors in shape but as we have said different in performance and dimensions.
The family is that of the XTs
In fact we have Xt30 - Xt60 - Xt90

Another important component for engaging and closing a 'electrical pole' properly is the heat-shrinkable sheath, which obviously should be RED or BLACK based on the welded post.

The electric cables must be welded to the two poles of the connector, I recommend to carry out excellent welding, it is worth the final result and the life of the cable itself. In addition to disconnecting one of the two poles it would immediately go short-circuiting with the opposite pole a few millimeters away.

COMMERCIAL CONNECTION plug

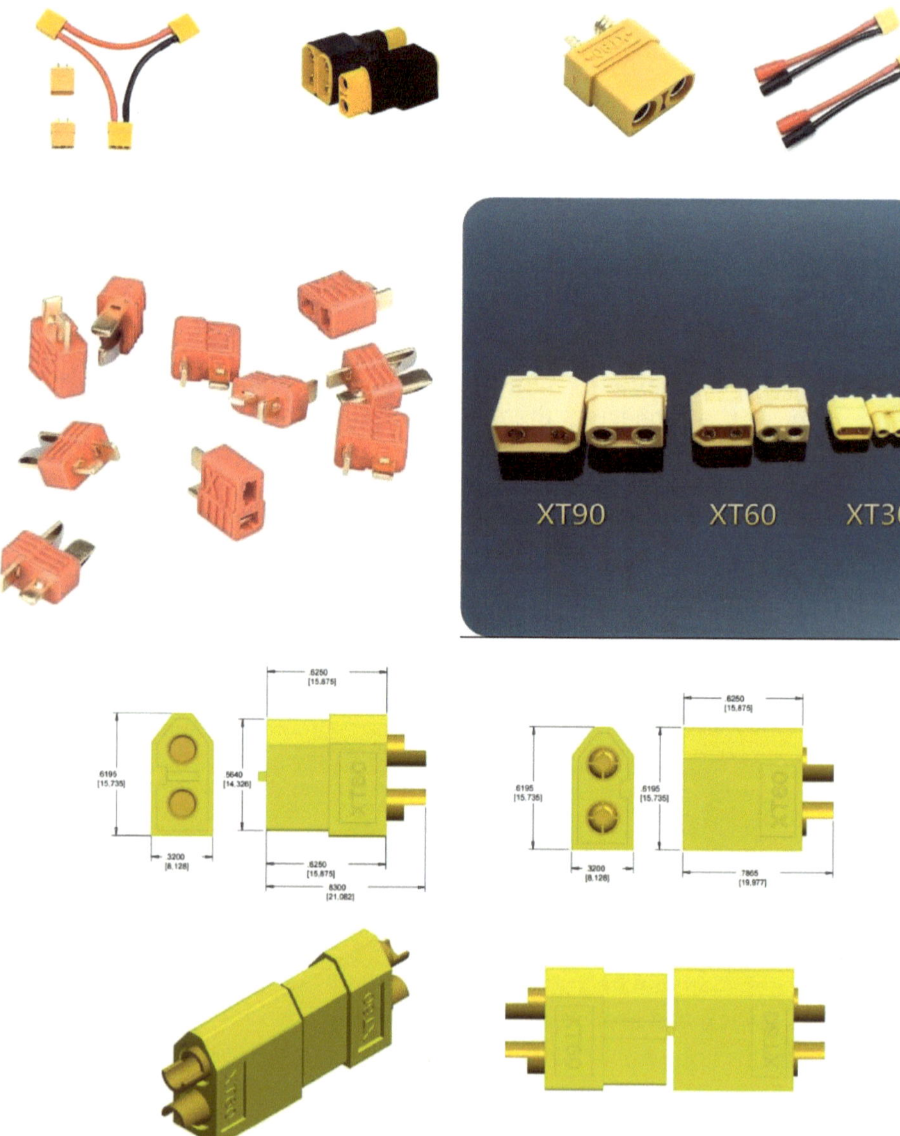

Useful advice on the choice:

The practical advice on choosing a pair of plug-in connectors is 3, the first advice is to go and look for the various technical data sheets of the various models, so as to have an effective idea of the real potential of the connector. An important fact is that of insulation and maximum current. I suggest two is to always oversize the connectors in your system, this if your motor has a maximum absorption of 50 A, try to install a plug-in connector that has a technical card over 70 Ampere. So as not to have overheating or other problems technical problems resulting from poor conductivity (the motor if the connector is small will never have the 50Ampere required on the label). I take into consideration the XT family because it is the one that has a higher quality / price ratio, very good in terms of build quality even if obviously they have a cost that exceeds other "economic" models.

Features of the 3 models:

The Model XT30 has a **MAX 30AMPERE** capacity
The Model XT60 has a maximum capacity of **60AMPERE**
The Model XT90 has a **MAX 90AMPERE** capacity

Medium and low power connectors

However, this series of plug-in connectors are also used to supply medium / low power loads. In fact a good part does not exceed a capacity of 2 Ampere The medium-low flow connectors are used on BMS and charge balancing boards, these connectors usually connected to BMS of various models have the task of recharging the battery packs with low currents in a balanced way (in the case of small battery packs).

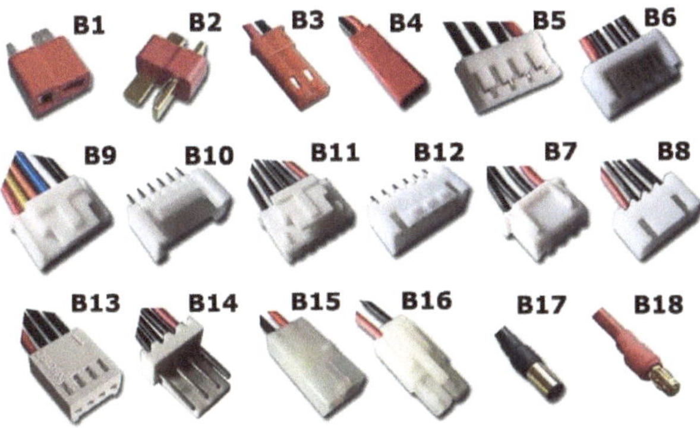

High performance connectors

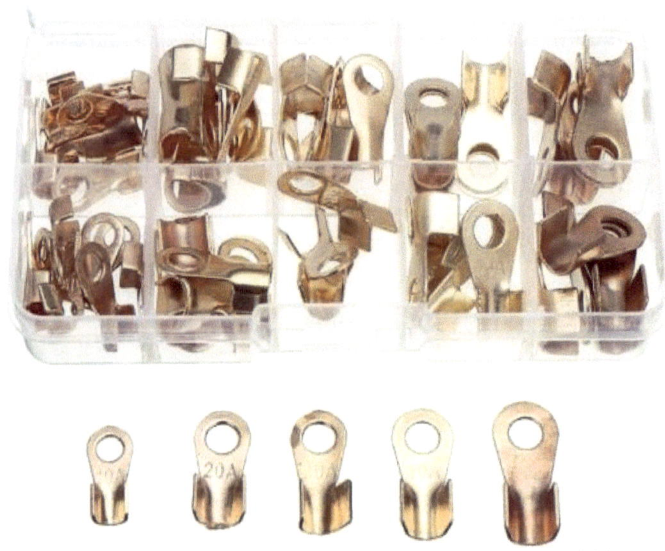

This connector alternative is not a real plug-in connector, but we can also integrate it in this small manual because for the correct high ones they are the best solution. In fact they also reach over 500AMPERE of continuous discharge. These too must be welded correctly and insulated with a heat-shrinkable sheath, the installation must be done with bolts and nuts of suitable diameter for optimal conductivity.

Final Recommendations:

It is recommended to use these connectors only if your system is compatible with a Plug system, the cables must be soldered and insulated to avoid water and vapor infiltration. Do not reverse the polarity at the time of welding. WARNING may cause short circuits in the circuit or in the battery. Test the soldered connector before connecting to the battery.

LITHIUM CELLS 18650

Dear Readers & Customers Friends, After receiving hundreds of requests for diagrams, guides and instructions today with this small but clear guide we want to welcome you and a special thank you for having purchased this book.

On the explicit request of the customer we can go to realize practical guides on battery packs with specific voltage for example: We will call them according to the model (XX S):
2s 3s 4s 5s 6s 7s 8s 9s 10s 11s 12s 13s 14s 15s 16s 17s 18s 19s 20s 21s and above.

Do you have questions? Do you want a customized guide that can give you the info you need? Ask for it at: Gf.elettronica@live.it -

1)   WHAT ARE THE 18650 CELLS
     2) WHICH COMPONENTS MAKE THEM
     3) WHAT ATTENTION FOR USE
     4) WHAT BRANDS AND HOW WE RECOGNIZE THEM

The 18650 lithium cells are rechargeable batteries with a standardized container and used all over the world, thanks to their small size / weight they are able to feed millions of portable devices every day. From your laptop PC to alarm clocks or even night flashlight. There are hundreds of cell 18650 variants on the market, what differs from cell to the production Brand and quality is the value of 'capacity'. The capacity of a cell shows us in TRUE how much energy that battery can collect inside it and with simple alcohols it will give us, based on the consumption of the equipment to be powered, the final result which is the duration in time "autonomy". The battery takes its name from its size, in fact it measures 18mm in diameter and 65mm in height. The weight varies from the quality of the cell itself, the higher the quality and the more capacity the cell will have, the more its weight will be.

LG	LGCS318650	18650	Blue	White	
LG	LGDA2E18650	18650	Grey	White	
LG	LGDA418650	18650	Yellow	White	
LG	LGDAHA11865 ICR18650HA1	18650	Green (Light)	White	
LG	LGDAHB21865 ICR18650HB2	18650	Teal	White	
LG	LGDAHB61865	18650	Red (Dark)	White	
LG	LGDAHD2C1865	18650	Peach	White	
LG	LGDAMF11865	18650	Purple	White	
LG	LGDAS31865 ICR18650S3	18650	Blue	White	
LG	LGDAS41865	18650	Purple (Dark)	White	
LG	LGDB118650 ICR18650B1	18650	Teal	White	
LG	LGDB218650 ICR18650B2	18650	Pink	White	
LG	LGDB218650 ICR18650B2	18650	Orange	White	
LG	LGDB318650	18650	Tan	White	
LG	LGDBB31865 ICR18650B3	18650	Purple (Dark)	White	
LG	LGDBB31865 ICR18650B3	18650	Salmon	White	
LG	LGDBB31865 ICR18650B3	18650	Tan	White	
LG	LGDBB41865 ICR18650B4	18650	Grey	White	
LG	LGDBC21865 ICR18650C2	18650	Orange	White	
LG	LGDBD11865 ICR18650D1	18650	Pink	White	
LG	LGDBHE21865 IMR18650HE2	18650	Red (Dark)	White	
LG	LGDBHE21865 IMR18650HE2	18650	Red	White	

LG	LGDBHE41865 INR18650HE4	18650	Yellow	White	
LG	LGDBHG21865 INR18650HG2	18650	Brown	White	
LG	LGDBMJ11865 INR18650MJ1	18650	Green	White	
LG	LGDC118650 ICR18650C1	18650	Brown	White	
LG	LGDS218650 ICR18650S2	18650	Peach	White	
LG	LGDS318650 ICR18650S3	18650	Blue	White	
LG	LGEAMF11865 ICR18650MF1	18650	Purple	White	
LG	LGEAS318650 ICR18650S3	18650	Blue	White	
LG	LGEBMF21865	18650	Purple (Dark)	White	
LG	LGEP218650	18650	Purple	White	
LG	LGES218650 ICR18650S2	18650	Peach	White	
LG	LGES318650	18650	Blue	White	
Lishen (LS)	IFR-18650EC	18650	Blue	White	
Lishen (LS)	IMR-26700AB	26700	Brown		
Lishen (LS)	LR18650SK	18650	Green	Blue (Light)	
Lishen (LS)	LR1865AH	18650	Purple (Light)	White	
Lishen (LS)	LR1865AM	18650	Yellow	Grey	
Lishen (LS)	LR1865BC	18650	Orange	White	
Lishen (LS)	LR1865LA	18650	Green	Grey	
Lishen (LS)	LR1865SF	18650	Gray	White	
Moli Energy	ICR-18650	18650	Turquoise	Black	
Moli Energy	ICR-18650G	18650	Grey	Black	

Moli Energy	ICR-18650H	18650	Yellow (Light)	Black
Moli Energy	ICR-18650J	18650	Purple	Blue (Dark)
Moli Energy	ICR-18650J	18650	Blue	Black
Moli Energy	ICR-18650K	18650	Purple	Blue (Dark)
Moli Energy	ICR-18650K	18650	Green	White
Moli Energy	ICR-18650M	18650	Purple	Black
Panasonic	CGR18650	18650	Pink	Black
Panasonic	CGR18650A	18650	Green (Light)	White
Panasonic	CGR18650AF	18650	Green	White
Panasonic	CGR18650C	18650	Blue	White
Panasonic	CGR18650CA	18650	Pink	Black
Panasonic	CGR18650CE	18650	Green (Light)	White
Panasonic	CGR18650CF	18650	Purple (Light)	White
Panasonic	CGR18650CG	18650	Green (Light)	White
Panasonic	CGR18650CH	18650	Gray	White
Panasonic	CGR18650D	18650	Teal (Light)	White
Panasonic	CGR18650DA	18650	Purple	White
Panasonic	CGR18650E	18650	Pink	White
Panasonic	CGR18650EA	18650	Green (Light)	White
Panasonic	CGR18650H	18650	Purple	Black
Panasonic	CGR18650HG	18650	Orange	Black
Panasonic	CGR18650HGL	18650	Purple (Dark)	Black
Panasonic	CGR18650HM	18650	Yellow	Black
Panasonic	NCR18650	18650	Gray	White
Panasonic	NCR18650A	18650	Green	White
Panasonic	NCR18650B	18650	Green (Light)	White

Panasonic	NCR18650BE	18650	Green (Light)	White
Panasonic	NCR18650D	18650	Gray	White
Panasonic	NCR18650PD	18650	Green (Light)	White
Panasonic	UR18650NSX	18650	Green	Light Brown
PKCELL	ICR18650-2200mAh	18650	Blue	Black
Samsung	ICR18650-18	18650	Green (Light)	White
Samsung	ICR18650-20	18650	Blue	White
Samsung	ICR18650-20B	18650	Blue (Light)	White
Samsung	ICR18650-20C	18650	Blue (Light)	White
Samsung	ICR18650-20F	18650	Blue (Light)	White
Samsung	ICR18650-22	18650	Teal	Blue (Light)
Samsung	ICR18650-22B	18650	Teal	Blue
Samsung	ICR18650-22E	18650	Teal	White
Samsung	ICR18650-22F	18650	Green	White
Samsung	ICR18650-22FM	18650	Green	White
Samsung	ICR18650-22FU	18650	Green	White
Samsung	ICR18650-22H	18650	Teal	White
Samsung	ICR18650-22P	18650	Purple (Light)	White
Samsung	ICR18650-24A	18650	Blue (Dark)	Blue
Samsung	ICR18650-24E	18650	Blue	White
Samsung	ICR18650-24F	18650	Green	White
Samsung	ICR18650-26A	18650	Pink	White
Samsung	ICR18650-26C	18650	Pink	White
Samsung	ICR18650-26D	18650	Pink	White
Samsung	ICR18650-26F	18650	Pink	White
Samsung	ICR18650-26FM	18650	Pink	White
Samsung	ICR18650-26FU	18650	Pink	White

Samsung	ICR18650-26H	18650	Pink	White		
Samsung	ICR18650-26J	18650	Pink	White		
Samsung	ICR18650-28A	18650	Purple (Light)	White		
Samsung	ICR18650-30A	18650	Purple (Light)	White		
Samsung	ICR18650-30B	18650	Green (Light)	White		
Samsung	ICR18650-30B	18650	Purple	White		
Samsung	ICR18650-32A	18650	Purple (Light)	White		
Samsung	INR18650-13B	18650	Purple	White		
Samsung	INR18650-13P	18650	Turquoise	White		
Samsung	INR18650-13Q	18650	Teal	White		
Samsung	INR18650-15M	18650	Blue (Light)	White		
Samsung	INR18650-15MM	18650	Blue (Light)	White		
Samsung	INR18650-15Q INR18650-15L	18650	Green (Light)	White		
Samsung	INR18650-15Q	18650	Teal	White		
Samsung	INR18650-15R	18650	Teal	White		
Samsung	INR18650-20Q	18650	Teal	White		
Samsung	INR18650-20R	18650	Teal	White		
Samsung	INR18650-25R	18650	Green	White		
Samsung	INR18650-25R	18650	Blue (Light)	White		
Samsung	INR18650-29E	18650	Purple (Light)	White		
Samsung	INR18650-30Q	18650	Purple	White		
Sanyo		18650	Red	Purple		

Sanyo		18650	Red	Blue	
Sanyo	NCR18650BF	18650	Red	Brown	
Sanyo	NCR18650BL	18650	Red	Black	
Sanyo	NCR18650GA	18650	Red	Blue	
Sanyo	UR18650A	18650	Red	White	
Sanyo	UR18650E	18650	Red	Purple (Grey)	
Sanyo	UR18650F R1122	18650	Red	Blue (Cyan)	
Sanyo	UR18650FB	18650	Red	Green	
Sanyo	UR18650FJ	18650	Red	Orange	
Sanyo	UR18650FK	18650	Red	Teal	
Sanyo	UR18650FM	18650	Red	Black	
Sanyo	UR18650H	18650	Red	Black	
Sanyo	UR18650RX	18650	Red	Blue	
Sanyo	UR18650S	18650	Red	Orange	
Sanyo	UR18650SA	18650	Red	Brown	
Sanyo	UR18650W2	18650	Red	Pink	
Sanyo	UR18650WX	18650	Red	Blue (Cyan)	
Sanyo	UR18650Y	18650	Red	Green (Light)	
Sanyo	UR18650ZT R1122	18650	Orange	Purple	
Sanyo	UR18650ZTA	18650	Purple	Yellow	
Sanyo	UR18650ZY	18650	Red	Purple (Light)	
Sinc	CRN18650-2200MAH	18650	Green		
SINC	ISR18650-2600MAH	18650	Pink	Grey (Light)	
Sony	<delete>	18650	Green	Black	
Sony	SF US18650V	18650	Green	Black	
Sony	US17670	18650	Blue (Dark)	Tan	
Sony	US18650E	18650	White	Black	
Sony	US18650FT	18650	Green	Black	

Sony	US18650GR (G2)	18650	Green	Black	
Sony	US18650GR (G3)	18650	Green	Black	
Sony	US18650GR (G4)	18650	Green	Black	

If you also have at least one of these cells and want to find out if it is of good quality or if it is an 'anonymous' production cell 'follow this list. You will find the specific color of the protective cover, the color of the positive pole card that is usually in light paper or cardboard, an indispensable component to avoid short circuits in the cell itself. The serial number / brand and year of production will tell you according to the specifications and the technical sheets we have available for those interested, they will tell you how much your cell's capacity, working voltages, currents, temperatures and lots of other important data are. Lithium 18650 False cells, be very careful about what you go to buy, there are hundreds of FAKE models on the market, fakes that sellers pass off as '' GOOD ''instead they are just FALSE CELLS.

POLO POSITIVO DELLE CELLE 18650

All the 18650 cells, enclose the plastic cover inside, on a positive pole a small circle of paper or cardboard, which has the purpose and very important task of keeping the cell body (negative) with the positive pole isolated.

As we know they are at a distance of a few mm from each other. A short circuit would cause serious damage to the cell and also to the operator who happens to be in the vicinity. In fact, when these cells are short-circuited they will go over and in less than a few seconds or minutes you will have an unloaded car with bursts and flames. All this also depends on cell to cell, there are good quality cells that adopt small tricks that minimize the explosion, but there are also low quality cells that in less than a few seconds explode like firecrackers. Let's also say that some

cells may be of good BRAND but can be "defective". This means that despite being of good quality they may not comply with the standards and safety standards of the parent company. This is a very difficult case, but it can always happen that we come across a cell "purchased at low cost but of good quality".

Another very important component of a 18650 cell is the cover, the cover exists in various colors and thicknesses, the standard however is a thermal film that after being inserted just a heat source to make it shrink and stick all around the cell carcass itself .

18650

This film is very important for safety, as it keeps the cell well INSULATED, its body is in fact all negative pole and it could happen that with other cells '' stripped of covers '' they give us a mega short circuit with possible explosions and flames. Don't forget to change the cover if there are tears or breakdowns! It is very important to always have it perfect on the whole surface!

THE DIMENSIONS OF THE 18650 CELL

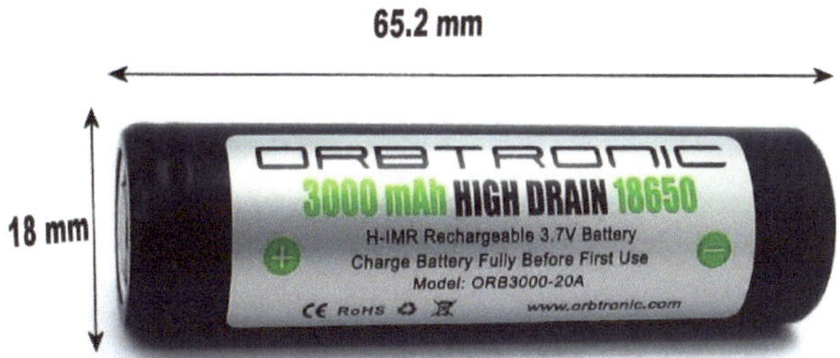

How is it made inside the cell?
The cell inside has a sheet a few meters long of insulating material flanked with semiconductor material, plus a liquid that keeps the electrolytic elements in a good state of life. This sheet, a few meters long, is rolled up

on itself, forming a soft cylinder, where in the central point we have the POSITIVE pole and in the external end point we have the NEGATIVE pole.

This will then be inserted into the metal container and will be connected to the carcass metal mass and the positive metal pole of the cell. The longer the sheet is, the more turns our conductor / insulator material will have, the heavier our cell will be and more obviously its storage capacity will be.

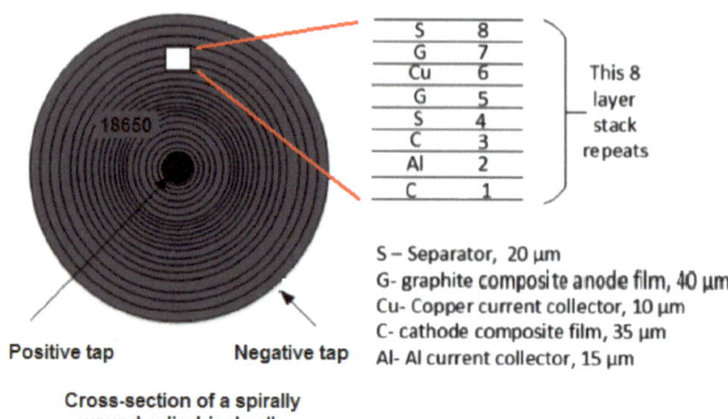

Cross-section of a spirally wound cylindrical cell

Cell capacity is measured in mah (milliamps / hour)

A Cell of good capacity goes from 2000 to 3500mah, however there are cells with a lower capacity, such as: 700mah-900mah-1000mah-1200mah.Excellent where great autonomy is not needed. Where instead you need autonomy there are also much more efficient cells! Obviously everything is proportional to the spending budget you have for your project. We have cells from: 3100mah-3200mah-**3500mah** is the best current cell on the market!

Obviously we are talking about Branded, original and quality cells. Since on foreign e-commerce we find anonymous cells with values that clearly exceed this threshold. But how are we going to see and as you could already understand from the video " fake cell " are just forgers selling low quality or low capacity products by inserting false labels. The 18650 cells as an important technical data sheet value must also be taken into consideration the maximum discharge current. In fact we have cells that are able to give current discharges under stress of more than 10/15/20 amperes. There are

cells for particular uses see (electronic cigarette) that are able to give impulses of more than 30 / 38A.

There are two alternatives for the positive pole, one is that of a flat pole at the level of the sheath and paper insulator, and the second is the 'protruding' one. From experience I tell you that you DO NOT have to go and spend money where the cell is a model SPORGENT as it is already a fact that makes us think of FAKE. The cells of good quality are all with positive PLATE, this is because the big companies are going to weld them with spot welders

SOME CELLS OF BUSINESS
FIND THE INTRUDER

TR18650   TR18650   UltraFire   SONY   SANYO   SAMSUNG   Momiji

IN THIS PHOTO WE HAVE 7 COMMERCIAL CELLS YOU CAN FIND IN THE MARKET, PLEASE CAREFULLY READ THE TARGA DATA. WHAT DO YOU KNOW IN STRANGE?

Electric cables Commercial section table

AWG	Diametro mm	Sezione (Area) mm2	AWG	Diametro mm	Sezione (Area) mm2
0000 (4/0)	11,684	107,22	21	0,723	0,411
000 (3/0)	10,405	85,01	22	0,644	0,324
00 (2/0)	9,266	67,43	23	0,573	0,259
0 (1/0)	8,252	53,49	24	0,511	0,205
1	7,348	42,41	25	0,455	0,162
2	6,544	33,62	26	0,405	0,128
3	5,827	26,67	27	0,361	0,102
4	5,189	21,15	28	0,321	0,0806
5	4,62	16,77	29	0,286	0,0649
6	4,115	13,3	30	0,255	0,0507
7	3,655	10,55	31	0,227	0,0401
8	3,264	8,37	32	0,202	0,0324
9	2,906	6,63	33	0,18	0,0255
10	2,588	5,26	34	0,16	0,0201
11	2,305	4,17	35	0,143	0,0159
12	2,052	3,31	36	0,127	0,0127
13	1,828	2,63	37	0,113	0,0103
14	1,623	2,08	38	0,101	0,0081
15	1,45	1,65	39	0,09	0,0062
16	1,291	1,31	40	0,08	0,0049
17	1,149	1,04	41	0,071	0,0039
18	1,024	0,823	42	0,064	0,0032
19	0,912	0,653	43	0,056	0,0025
20	0,812	0,519	44	0,051	0,0020

The most used conductors with specific maximum currents:

AWG	Dia mm	SWG	Dia mm	Max Amps	Ohms / 100 m
11	2.30	13	2.34	12	0.47
12	2.05	14	2.03	9.3	0.67
13	1.83	15	1.83	7.4	0.85
14	1.63	16	1.63	5.9	1.07
15	1.45	17	1.42	4.7	1.35
16	1.29	18	1.219	3.7	1.48
18	1.024	19	1.016	2.3	2.04
19	0.912	20	0.914	1.8	2.6
20	0.812	21	0.813	1.5	3.5
21	0.723	22	0.711	1.2	4.3
22	0.644	23	0.610	0.92	5.6
23	0.573	24	0.559	0.729	7.0
24	0.511	25	0.508	0.577	8.7
25	0.455	26	0.457	0.457	10.5
26	0.405	27	0.417	0.361	13.0
27	0.361	28	0.376	0.288	15.5
28	0.321	30	0.315	0.226	22.1
29	0.286	32	0.274	0.182	29.2
30	0.255	33	0.254	0.142	34.7
31	0.226	34	0.234	0.113	40.2
32	0.203	36	0.193	0.091	58.9
33	0.180	37	0.173	0.072	76.7
34	0.160	38	0.152	0.056	94.5
35	0.142	39	0.132	0.044	121.2

THE FUSES - COMMERCIAL MODELS

There are hundreds of models, sizes, shapes and reference currents on the market. The fuse is an electrical protection component that is mounted in all electrical systems as a protection component, in fact it protects us from short circuits. But how do fuses work?

Very simple! Fuses that are made of glass, ceramic, plastic etc. They have an external container, which gives it its shape and color, but internally the technology is always the same. In fact, we have a strip of conductive material, which allows us to slide the electrons and power our user. In fact, we can power LED lights, motors, halogen lamps, and electronic circuits in general. The fuse must generally be inserted on the positive pole of the power cable, when the current passes the fuse does not oppose, but if the technical data sheet threshold is exceeded, the conductive foil overheats, the temperatures rise, it becomes incandescent until it it burns. Burning interrupts the circuit, that is, it has protected our charge from an overload.

Example:

We have an electric motor + a lithium battery

To power our electric motor what maximum can absorb 50Apere what should we do? We are going to put a fuse of 50Amp as plate data, so any extra current will be perceived by the fuse as beyond the standard and it will burn. It is also possible to use fuses with values lower than the maximum indicated on the motor or user plate data, for example one of 10 AMP/20AMP/30AMP etc. What happens when lower values are used? That if your motor has a need for current beyond the threshold of the fuse, the latter will burn out, even if the specific motor can also go well beyond 10 or 20 AMPS. This happens if our motor is installed for example on an electric bike, in a standard distance without climbs, slopes we have for example a current absorption of 20AMPER, when we start to make the climb, and the higher this is the more the engine will struggle to push you and the more the demand for current you can get even over 50 ° for example of the technical data sheet of the motor. As you understand these power surges are not good for cables if they are poorly sized, and not even for lithium battery cards, but it is the same as lead or gel batteries, which all boast very high pulse currents even over 200 / 300AMPERE.

This example also applies to a photovoltaic system where, as the right rule, a fuse must be positioned at the input and output of the charge regulator, so as to protect both upstream and downstream of it. The fuses are used in cars, motorcycles, traditional scooters, we also find them in quality products such as appliances, electric bikes, electric scooters, TVs, monitors, computers and much more. The aim is always to protect the circuit downstream of the fuse, even if they operate at low, medium or high voltage. In fact, in TVs and 230v users the fuses are sized for low currents even mA (milliamps) and work precisely.

The higher the voltage, the less current we will have in our system, vice versa in the case of low voltage systems, see 12v of cars! The fuses have very high current values, such as 5-10-20-30-50-100AMPERE. If then we also go to the AUDIOFILO sector, therefore amplifiers, high-performance batteries, the currents exceed abundantly even 200 / 300AMPERE

HIGH AMPERE FUSES

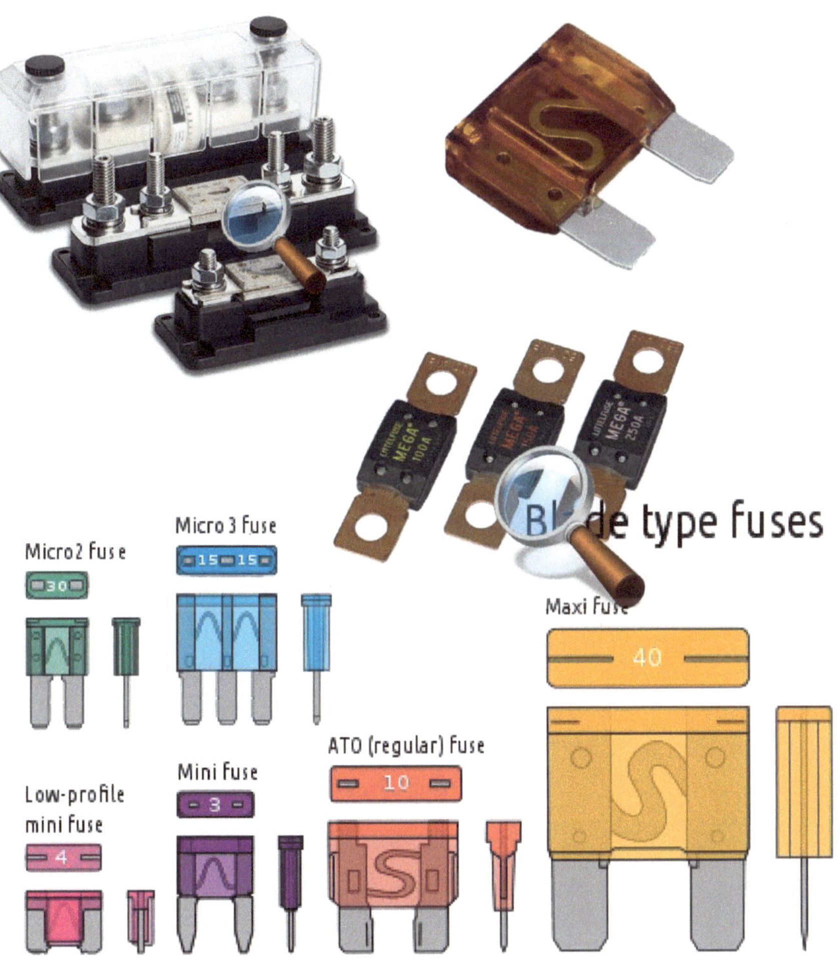

LOW AMPERE FUSES

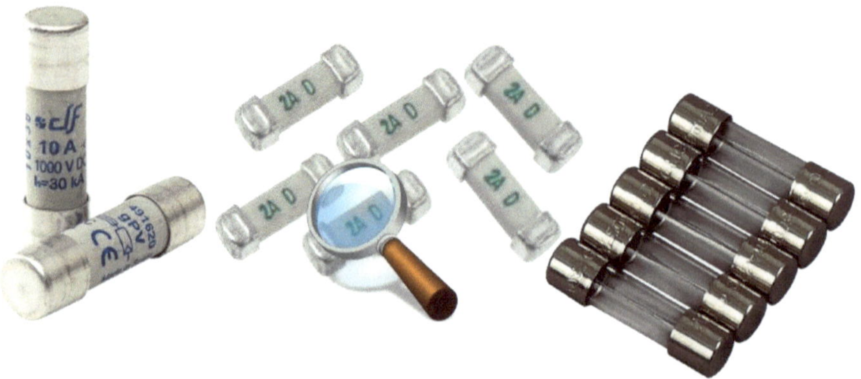

Having seen some fuse models that you can easily find in any electricity / electronics shop, let's analyze the operation. These are USA and DISPOSABLE components, precisely because when they start operating they burn and can no longer be reused. Then there is another category of fuse, more complex and used in particular applications, it is precisely the self-resetting fuses. These components are used in the same way as the fuses that we are analyzing in these files, with the only difference that the internal foil after a period of " rest " returns to the starting position again. Returning to the position again allows the circuit to function as per standard, and obviously its operation will repeat itself over and over again. This will save you the boredom of replacing the fuses manually, purchasing them, and of remaining " in the dark " with the equipment that protected. Obviously, however, the cost of a normal fuse is really really low, instead the self-resetting ones that are in a special category! they are much taller. An example of short circuit protection that is self-restoring or better that protects you but then you can go and have it functioned again is our lifesaver in the apartment or garage. What does this do? It trips as soon as an overload or a short circuit is detected, but obviously the reactivation is not automatic for safety reasons you will have to go to reset the switch and run energy again to your system (after obviously eliminating the cause of the malfunction that triggered the RCD).

If you want more info on how your home's lifesaver works, I want to remind you that there is a booklet entirely dedicated to him. You will find info, technical notions and many tips on use.

SELF-RESETTING FUSES

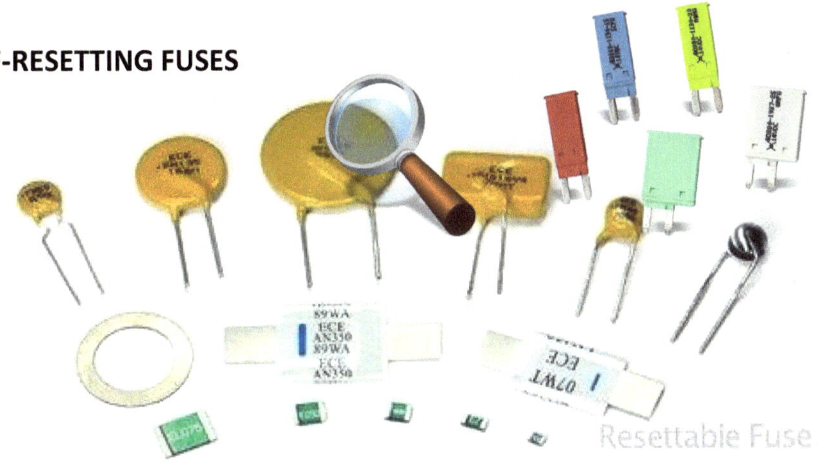

SUPER FUSE 500A

ELECTRICAL DIAGRAM WITH THE USE OF THE FUSE

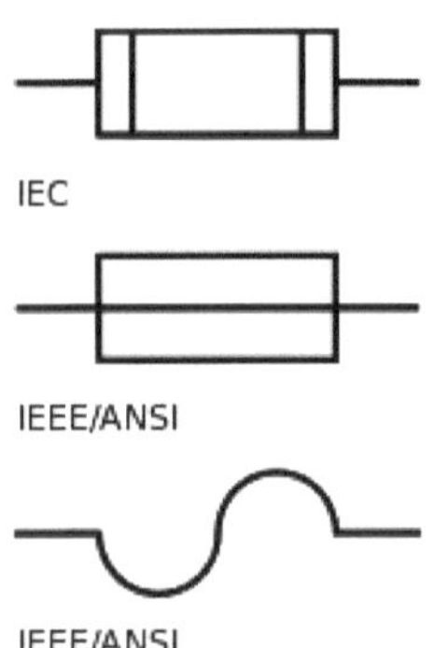

The electrical symbol of the fuse varies according to the models, these three are a practical example. It also varies from the symbology corresponding to

Institute of Electrical and Electronics Engineers,

International Electrotechnical Commission

American National Standards Institute.

ELECTRICAL DIAGRAM WITH FUSE

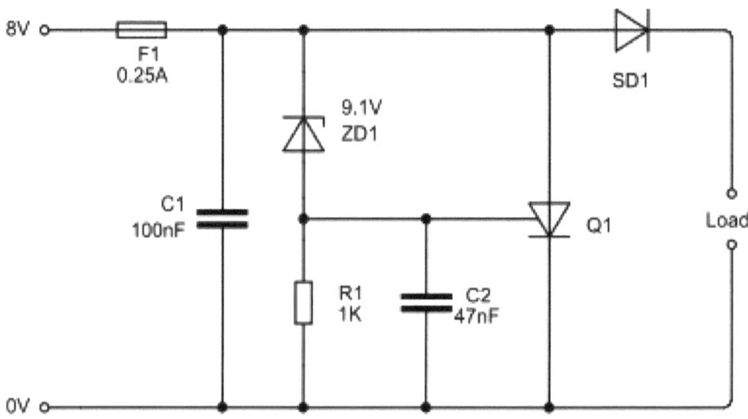

This is a very simple electrical diagram where you can find the fuse, as you can see and as already mentioned above, they must be inserted on the POSITIVE poles of the circuit power supply, whether they are electrical or electronic circuits (PCB). In this scheme the fuse is the component called F1 from 0.25AMP. The operating voltage of the whole circuit is 8v and the maximum power allowed for the load is 2w. If the load or the circuit downstream of the fuse has an absorption beyond these 0.250mA, the fuse burns out, protecting everything automatically. If a self-resetting fuse is used, everything will restart after a short time (if there is still no short circuit downstream) or if it is a standard fuse it must be replaced with a new one with the same electrical characteristics.

Color scheme (for mini and medium):

Color	Flow
Black	1A (first medium)
Grey	2A
Violet	3A
Rose	4A
Orange	5A
Brown	7.5A
Red	10A
Light blue	15A
Yellow	20A
Transparent	25A
Green	30A
Green-Blue	35A (first medium)
Amber	40A (first medium)

Large size fuse colors

Colore	Flow
Yellow	20A
Grey	25A (rarely used)
Green	30A
Brown	35A (rarely used)
Orange	40A
Red	50A
Light blue	60A
Orange	70A
Transparent	80A
Violet	100A

THERMAL FUSES

There are also thermal fuses, which as the word TEMPERATURE itself says. These fuses trip not with the variation of the current in the internal filament but with the increase in the temperature of the component to be kept under control. For example we have an electric motor that must not go beyond 50 ° C, we are going to insert a thermal fuse on the positive power pole and this will burn out or better open the circuit (protecting the motor) from a temperature beyond that from the Card technique. A further use can be on the use of electric heaters for heating, once a temperature threshold is exceeded, the circuit is interrupted, the resistors are cut off current so as to stay below the limit threshold.
The thermal fuses are also called TCO ranging from about 50 to 300 ° C, there are also for this model of fuse resettable types, manually forcing the foil in working position and not AUTO restoring as in the past model.

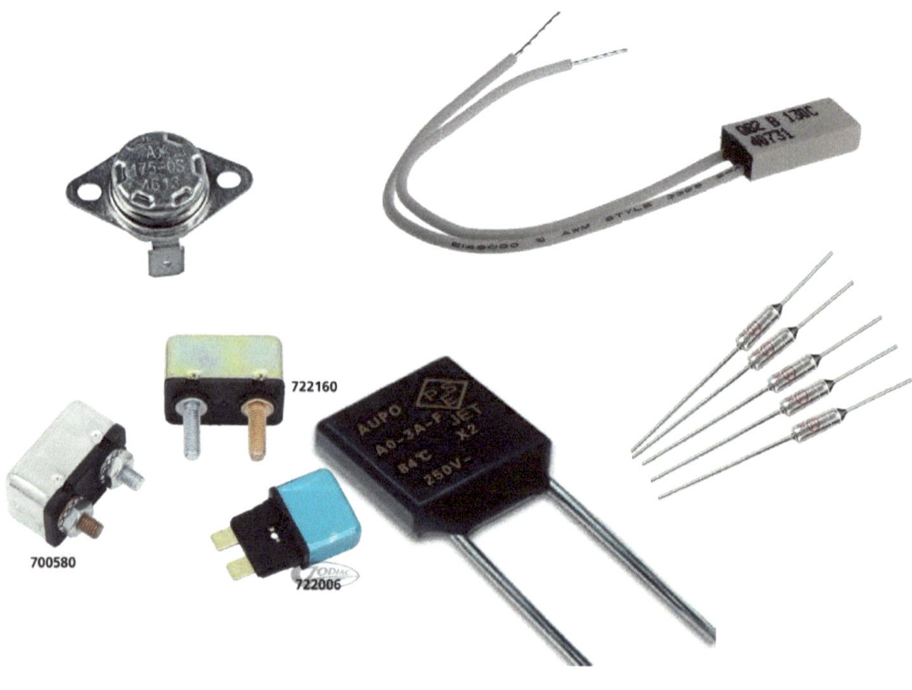

Easy-to-use commercial solutions, Standard fuses

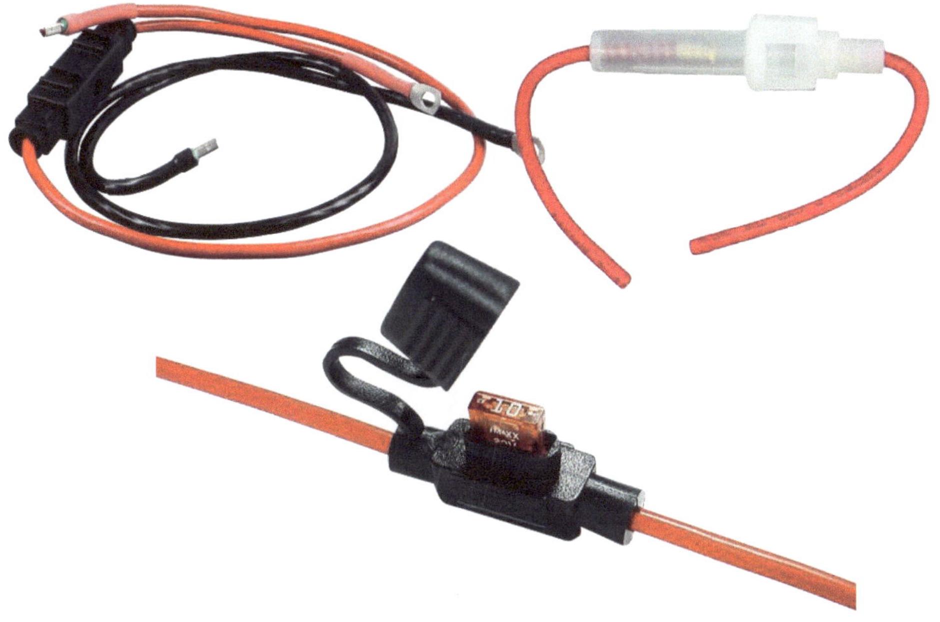

This guide ends here, I invite you to leave a 5 star positive Feedback and maybe a photo, with your comment on Amazon!

Do not forget that you can find more dossiers also of other topics directly online, fast and free shipping thanks to Amazon Prime!

And remember that the only GFE files are these!

This guide ends here, I invite you to leave a positive 5-star feedback and maybe a photo, with your comment on Amazon!
Don't forget that you can find more files on other topics directly online, fast and free shipping thanks to Amazon Prime!
And remember that the only GFE files are these!